DAVID ORTIZ

WORLD SERIES CHAMPION

RYAN NAGELHOUT

Britannica®
Educational Publishing

IN ASSOCIATION WITH

ROSEN
EDUCATIONAL SERVICES

Published in 2016 by Britannica Educational Publishing (a trademark of Encyclopædia Britannica, Inc.) in association with The Rosen Publishing Group, Inc.
29 East 21st Street, New York, NY 10010

Distributed exclusively by Rosen Publishing.
To see additional Britannica Educational Publishing titles, go to rosenpublishing.com.

First Edition

Britannica Educational Publishing
J.E. Luebering: Director, Core Reference Group
Anthony L. Green: Editor, Compton's by Britannica

Rosen Publishing
Kathy Campbell: Editor
Nelson Sá: Art Director
Brian Garvey: Designer
Cindy Reiman: Photography Manager

Library of Congress Cataloging-in-Publication Data

Nagelhout, Ryan.
David Ortiz: World Series Champion/Ryan Nagelhout.—First Edition.
        pages cm.—(Living Legends of Sports)
"Distributed exclusively by Rosen Publishing"—T.p. verso.
Includes bibliographical references and index.
ISBN 978-1-68048-099-3 (Library bound)—ISBN 978-1-68048-100-6 (Paperback)—ISBN 978-1-68048-102-0 (6-pack)
1. Ortiz, David, 1975-—Juvenile literature. 2. Baseball players—Dominican Republic—Biography—Juvenile literature. I. Title.
GV865.O78N34 2015
796.3570922—dc23
[B]
2014039834

Manufactured in the United States of America

CONTENTS

BALL   STRIKE   OUT — H — E

INTRO-DUCTION

When sports fans think of great Boston Red Sox players, they look to the numbers hanging over right field in the city's historic Fenway Park. Ted Williams's number 9, Carl Yastrzemski's 8, or Jim Rice's 14 were all retired by the Red Sox following those players' spectacular careers with the team. For more than a century, fans have filled Fenway Park to see the greats of the game dazzle them with towering home runs and important victories.

Today's Red Sox fans fill the stands at Fenway to see one living

David Ortiz is one of the most feared hitters in baseball. His number 34 will likely join the numbers of seven other Boston Red Sox players that have been retired.

legend play: David Ortiz. The designated hitter (DH) known as Big Papi has wowed Red Sox fans with big hits and an even bigger smile for more than a decade. Whether sitting atop the park's iconic thirty-seven-foot (eleven-meter) tall left-field wall, nicknamed the Green Monster, or cheering from the centerfield bleachers, everyone in Fenway Park hopes to get a home run ball when Ortiz steps to the plate.

In 2004, Ortiz's big bat led the Red Sox to their first World Series championship in eighty-six years. His clutch hitting helped Boston win two more championships over the next decade and solidified his reputation as one of the best big-game players in Major League Baseball history.

CHAPTER ONE

Growing Up Papi

David Américo Ortiz Arias was born on November 18, 1975, in the city of Santo Domingo in the Dominican Republic. Ortiz's parents, Enrique Ortiz and Angela Rosa Arias, had two children—David and his sister, Albania.

Ortiz's father was a baseball player, a pitcher, growing up. When Enrique and Angela got married and had David, Enrique stopped playing baseball and sold auto parts to take care of his family. Enrique taught David a lot about baseball, and Ortiz said his father helped him throughout his career in the major leagues.

Angela Rosa Arias worked as a secretary in the Dominican Republic's Department of Agriculture. She also traveled all over the Caribbean selling clothes and trying to make extra money for the family. When Ortiz was fourteen or fifteen years old, he and his family left Santo Domingo and moved to a town called Haina. Going from a city of nearly three million to the much smaller Haina was a big change for the family. The house was very small and the streets were not paved. There, with not much to do, Ortiz was constantly playing baseball.

QUICK FACT

The Dominican Republic shares the island of Hispaniola with the country of Haiti.

These children are playing baseball in the Dominican Republic. Cubans first brought baseball to the Dominican Republic in the 1880s and early 1890s.

Learning the Game

Baseball is the national sport of the Dominican Republic. Many great baseball players have grown up in the Dominican Republic and had long major league careers. Ortiz learned how to play baseball on the streets of Santo Domingo, which meant he was not playing with the equipment many baseball players are used to.

Ortiz said he never played baseball with a glove when he was growing up. His friends often did not have baseballs or bats either. He said he usually played with a broomstick as a bat, and a bottle cap as a ball. Sometimes he would steal a sock from his father and wrap it in a plastic bag. He would even break the heads off his sister's dolls and use them as baseballs.

Third baseman Adrián Beltré is another Major League Baseball (MLB) player who grew up in the Dominican Republic. He and Ortiz played together on the Red Sox in 2010.

Hitting a bottle cap with a broomstick is no easy task, but Ortiz thinks it helped him become a better hitter. "I have to believe it helped me develop my hand-eye coordination," Ortiz wrote in his 2007 autobiography, *Big Papi*. "I've always been able to hit a curveball, and I think one of the big reasons is because I learned how to hit a bottle cap with a broomstick when I was growing up."

QUICK FACT

The Dominican Republic has a population of just over ten million and is home to many major league stars, including Jose Reyes, Manny Ramirez, Robinson Canó, and Adrian Beltre.

When Ortiz was a teenager, his parents split up. David and Albania lived with their mother while his father remarried and had another child, David's half-sister, Yacili. Despite not living with his father, David continued to receive help from him and grew as a baseball player. His father drove up to watch David play and helped him draw the interest of major league teams.

BALL STRIKE OUT (H) (E)

MLB scouts rely on the knowledge of *buscones* and local scouts to get information about potential major leaguers in the Dominican Republic.

The *Buscones*

David played baseball and basketball for Estudia Espallat High School. While playing there, he got the attention of *buscones*, or street agents who help major league clubs scout players in the Dominican Republic. These *buscones* help players work out and get tryouts with teams. Sometimes they are former players themselves or they have friends in the United States who work for major league teams. *Buscones* give players equipment and whatever they need to play baseball, then get paid if a player signs a major league contract. *Buscones* have their players work out together in a group they call the Program.

Ortiz started working with a *buscón* when he was a teenager, working out at a field near his mother's house in Haina. In the Dominican Republic, you cannot sign with a club until you are sixteen years old. A scout named Edmundo Borreme, who worked for the Florida Marlins, had Ortiz work out with him and a few other players

Prospects working with the same buscón often practice and play together while major league teams scout them.

QUICK FACT

In 1992, the Florida Marlins were an expansion team. They had not even played a game yet when they were scouting Ortiz.

AT BAT   BALL   STRIKE OUT   (H)   (E)

for four or five months before Ortiz hurt his elbow.

Ortiz was sent home to rest his elbow, but a few months later another *buscón* named Hector Alvarez asked him to come play with his Program in Santo Domingo. Alvarez got in touch with a scout for the Seattle Mariners named Ramón de los Santos. Santos liked what he saw from Ortiz and had him come take batting practice in the Dominican Summer League.

On November 28, 1992, about two weeks after Ortiz turned seventeen, he signed a professional contract with the Seattle Mariners. Ortiz got a $7,500 signing bonus from the Mariners. He was officially a professional baseball player!

CHAPTER TWO

Going Pro

Making a major league club is no easy task. Even after you sign a contract with a major league team, you have to go through their minor league system and improve as a player. Major league teams sign young players hoping they will grow into great players, but it takes time. Many players put in years of work in the minor leagues and never make it to a big club.

Ortiz started his time with the Mariners in the Dominican Summer League before coming to the United States to play for Seattle's low Class A teams in Peoria, Arizona, in 1994. He played two seasons in Peoria before finally making the move up to high Class A ball in Wisconsin, in the Midwest League.

In his autobiography, Ortiz said the hardest part about moving to the United States was getting used to the food. He was a big fan of his mother's cooking, and much of the food in the Dominican Republic is very spicy. Ortiz said everything he ate in the United States tasted too sweet. Often he would find other players from the Dominican Republic and eat food at their houses. When Ortiz joined the Red Sox, he would

Ortiz was in the Mariners farm system for only three years before being traded to the Minnesota Twins.

often visit Pedro Martinez's sister and eat dinner with other players there.

David played 129 games for the Wisconsin Timber Rattlers in 1996, hitting eighteen home runs and batting .322 with the club. He thought he had a good season, which is why he was surprised when Seattle told him he had been traded. Ortiz was "a player to be named later" in a trade that happened between Seattle and the Minnesota Twins on August 29, 1996. Two weeks later, Ortiz was sent to Minnesota in exchange for Dave Hollins.

Breaking Through

At first, Ortiz was upset about the trade. His father helped him understand that it could be a good thing. He said the trade meant that Minnesota wanted him. It meant he was scouted by the Twins and they liked what they saw. Now it was time for him to prove them right.

He worked hard after the trade, moving from high Class A ball in Fort Myers, Florida, to start the season all the way to the majors. After sixty-one games in Fort Myers, Ortiz was promoted to AA New Britain, where he hit .322 in sixty-nine games. Ortiz was called up again, this time to AAA Salt Lake City of the Pacific Coast League. He played eleven games there before finally getting a late-season call-up from the Minnesota Twins.

Ortiz played fifteen games for the Twins in 1997, making his major league debut on September 2, against the Chicago Cubs. He got his first career hit, a double, against the Cubs the next night. On September 14, against the Texas Rangers, he hit his first career major league home run. Ortiz was the Twins' minor league player of the year in 1997, and he hoped to stay in the majors all season.

Today Ortiz is known for his big swing and long home runs, but Minnesota did not always want him swinging for the fences when he was

Big Papi was much thinner during his time with the Twins. They wanted him to be a speedy doubles hitter instead of a home run hitter.

QUICK FACT

Minnesota's 2001 postseason appearance was the team's first trip to the play-offs since winning the World Series in 1991.

at the plate. He says coaches in Minnesota tried to change his swing to make him hit more doubles and play baseball differently from how he was taught growing up.

Ortiz started the 1998 season with the Twins but spent some of the spring in Salt Lake City, Utah, with the Buzz. He played eighty-six games with the Twins, hitting .277 with nine home runs and sixty-three RBIs (runs batted in). He mostly played first base with Minnesota but also played as a DH. Despite finding some success in the majors, he played only ten games with the Twins in 1999. Ortiz played 130 games with Salt Lake City, hitting .315 with thirty home runs and 110 RBIs. The next year Ortiz played only in the majors, playing 130 games and hitting ten home runs and forty-six (RBIs) with a .282 batting average for Minnesota in 2000.

The 2001 season was hard for Ortiz. He hurt his wrist in May, but tried to play through it. On May 4, he had three hits, including a home run, but left the game with what turned out to be a broken wrist. Ortiz spent a few months rehabilitating in the minors and played only eighty-nine games with the Twins in 2001. He

Ortiz's home run numbers improved each season that he played with the Twins, from 1997 to 2002. Minnesota switched Ortiz to DH in 1999 to let him focus more on his hitting.

hit eighteen home runs and forty-eight RBIs, with a .234 batting average.

Ortiz's mother, Angela, died in a car accident on New Year's Day in 2002. It was a tragic start to a year that would change Ortiz's life in a big way. Ortiz hit a then-career-high twenty home runs with the Twins, batting .272 with seventy-five RBIs in 125 games. He also made it to the play-offs with Minnesota for the first time. Ortiz had eight hits in nine play-off games with the Twins, who lost to the Anaheim Angels in the American League Championship Series (ALCS).

David Ortiz thought he was finally becoming a major league star, but on December 16, 2002, the Twins released him from his contract. Ortiz was shocked. He was twenty-seven years old and without a job. Minnesota told him they might have to do something with his contract or possibly trade him, but he did not expect to be released.

Going to Boston

One day during the offseason, Ortiz saw Pedro Martinez at a restaurant. Martinez was the best pitcher on the Boston Red Sox, and he helped persuade Boston to sign Ortiz that winter. He thought Ortiz would be a good fit for the club, who needed help at first base and could use another good hitter for their lineup.

Ortiz was an instant hit in the Red Sox locker room. It is actually where he got the nickname Big Papi.

Ortiz and fellow slugger Manny Ramirez became one of the most feared number three and number four hitters in the game for opposing pitchers.

Ortiz often talked to other people in the locker room by calling them *papi*, a term that means "buddy" or "pal" in the Dominican Republic. It also means "pop" or "daddy," too. Standing at six feet four inches (2 m) and officially listed at 230 pounds (104 kilograms) the "big" David Ortiz said *papi* so often that his teammates called him "Big Papi," and the name stuck.

In Boston, Ortiz quickly became one of the best hitters on the team. Often batting just after Manny Ramirez in the Red Sox order, he clobbered thirty-one home runs and batted .288 in 2003. He also had 101 RBIs and played in 128 games as a DH. With the powerful batting duo of Ortiz and Ramirez, the Red Sox batted .289, the best in the

Ortiz's breakout season in 2003 helped the Red Sox get within a game of their first World Series appearance since 1986.

majors. Boston finished second in the American League East division behind the New York Yankees, which got them into the play-offs as a wild card team.

In the American League Division Series (ALDS), Boston played against the Oakland Athletics. The A's won the first two games of the five-game series, including a twelve-inning, game one win. However, Boston won the next three games to win the series and set

up a meeting with the Yankees in the ALCS. The series was a seven-game epic, with the teams splitting the first six games to force a game seven at Yankee Stadium. Ortiz hit a home run in that game, his second of the series, and the Red Sox took a 5–2 lead into the bottom of the eighth inning. However, the Yankees staged a furious comeback to tie the game. In the bottom of the eleventh inning, Yankees third baseman Aaron Boone hit the first pitch from Red Sox pitcher Tim Wakefield into the left field bleachers to send the Yankees to the World Series.

CHAPTER THREE

Comebacks and Championships

Ortiz and his teammates were crushed by the loss to the Yankees in 2003, but they did not give up. In 2004, Boston went 98–64 and once again won the wild card berth into the American League (AL) play-offs. Ortiz had another great regular season, hitting forty-one home runs and 139 RBIs while drawing seventy-five walks.

The 2004 Red Sox were a fun team to play for. With new manager Terry Francona, they called themselves "a bunch of idiots" who were trying to rewrite history and give Boston its first World Series title in more than eighty years. Along with players such as centerfielder Johnny Damon and first baseman Kevin Millar, Ortiz and fellow slugger Ramirez were considered the core of the "idiots," while Pedro Martinez and Curt Schilling led the pitching staff.

The Red Sox won three straight games to sweep Anaheim in the ALDS. Ortiz drove in the series-clinching runs with a two-run home run in the bottom of the tenth inning of game three, giving the Red Sox an 8–6 win to send Boston back to the ALCS. Meanwhile, the Yankees beat Minnesota in their divisional series, meaning the two rivals would face

Many people credited new manager Terry Francona with managing the big personalities of players like Ortiz, Manny Ramirez, and Pedro Martinez while giving the Red Sox a more relaxed clubhouse personality.

Ortiz and the Sox went into the series looking for revenge, but the Yankees won the first two games at Yankee Stadium against Boston's top two pitchers, Schilling and Martinez. Game three at Fenway Park was a disaster for Boston, a 19–8 blowout that put the Red Sox on the brink of elimination for the second straight season. No team in baseball had ever won four straight games to win a series when they trailed 3–0. Many people thought it was impossible.

Ortiz hit a two-run single in the bottom of the fifth inning to give the Red Sox a 2–1 lead in game four, but the Yankees would take a 4–3 lead into the ninth inning for their closer, Mariano Rivera. That is where the Red Sox comeback started, with Millar working a walk against Rivera. Dave Roberts came on as a pinch runner to steal second base, just getting under Yankee's shortstop Derek Jeter's tag. Three pitches later, third baseman Bill Mueller hit a single to center field to score Roberts and tie the game.

Three innings later, with the game still tied at 4 in the twelfth, Ortiz came up to bat against New York pitcher Paul Quantrill. With Ramirez on first after a single, Ortiz crushed a 2–1 pitch over the right field wall into the early morning Boston air to give the Red Sox a 6–4 win.

Boston won again the next night thanks to more heroics from Big Papi. Ortiz had an RBI single in the first inning to give Boston an early lead, but once again the game went into extra innings. Ortiz homered in the eighth to cut the Yankees lead to 4–3, and Rivera blew another save for the Yankees. In the fourteenth inning, with Johnny Damon on second base, Ortiz ripped a 2–2 pitch

QUICK FACT

Only four other teams in major professional sports history have overcome 3–0 deficits in a seven-game series, all in the National Hockey League: the 1942 Toronto Maple Leafs, 1975 New York Islanders, 2010 Philadelphia Flyers, and 2014 Los Angeles Kings.

Ortiz's two-run home run in the twelfth inning of game four of the 2004 ALCS remains one of the biggest hits in Big Papi's career.

from Esteban Loaiza into center field to drive in Damon and give the Red Sox a 5–4 win, sending the series back to New York.

In game six Ortiz went hitless but Boston scored four runs in the fourth to hang on to a 4–2 win, tying the series at three and forcing

An estimated crowd of three million people attended the Red Sox victory parade in 2004 as the team celebrated its first World Series win in eighty-six years.

game seven. On October 20, 2004, the Red Sox finally got their revenge. Boston beat New York 10–3 in game seven to reach the World Series for the first time since 1986. Ortiz hit a two-run home run in the first inning off Kevin Brown to start the offense, and Damon's grand slam

in the second all but put the game out of reach.

Ortiz had twelve hits—including three home runs—eleven RBIs, and was named the series most valuable player (MVP). The series changed Big Papi from an ordinary home run-hitting desig-nated hitter to one of the most feared postseason hitters ever to play the game. Boston went on to sweep the St. Louis Cardinals in the World Series, winning its first championship in eighty-six years. Ortiz hit a first-inning home run in game one at Fenway Park and fin-ished the series with four hits, four RBIs, and four walks. He

QUICK FACT

Game five of the 2004 ALCS is tied for the fifth-longest play-off baseball game in major league history.

AT BAT · BALL · STRIKE OUT Ⓗ Ⓔ

even made a great defensive play in game three. Ortiz caught Jeff Suppan between third base and home in the third inning for a double play, helping Pedro Martinez hang on for the win.

Records and a Second Title

The Red Sox did not repeat as World Series champions in 2005, but Ortiz had an even better statistical season in Boston. He hit .300 with forty-seven home runs and a career-best 148 RBIs with the Red Sox, who lost to the Chicago White Sox in a three-game sweep in the ALCS. Ortiz made his second-straight All-Star Game and also won his third straight Silver Slugger award.

QUICK FACT

The Silver Slugger is an award given to the top offensive player at each position of the American and National Leagues by the manufacturer of the Louisville Slugger bats.

Boston missed the play-offs altogether in 2006, but Ortiz set even more records with the Red Sox. Along with another Silver Slugger award and an All-Star appearance, Ortiz hit fifty-four home runs, breaking the previous Red Sox record of 50 set by Jimmie Foxx in 1938. Ortiz's batting average dropped a bit, down to .287, but he led the American League in home runs and RBIs (137) while walking an AL-best 119 times.

Only a few players from the 2004 World Series championship team were still on the Red Sox by 2007. Pedro Martinez left Boston, who traded with the Florida Marlins to get pitcher Josh Beckett and third baseman Mike Lowell. Young players such as center fielder Jacoby Ellsbury and second baseman Dustin Pedroia came in and made a huge difference with the team.

Ortiz hit only thirty-five home runs in 2007, but with 111 walks he had a league-best .445 on-base percentage. Boston took the AL East division lead on April 18 and never looked back, rolling to a

Sluggers often strike out a lot trying to hit home runs, but drawing walks and getting on base is an important way for a baseball player to help his team's offense score runs.

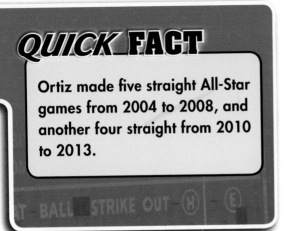

QUICK FACT

Ortiz made five straight All-Star games from 2004 to 2008, and another four straight from 2010 to 2013.

96–66 record and an AL East title. The Red Sox swept the Los Angeles Angels of Anaheim in the ALDS. Ortiz had a huge series for the Sox, getting five hits in three games, including a pair of home runs. He drove in three RBIs and walked six times!

Boston had to make another comeback in the ALCS, overcoming a 3–1 series deficit against the Cleveland Indians to make the World Series for the second time in four seasons. Ortiz had seven hits in the series, with a home run, three RBIs, and six walks. In the 2007 World Series, Boston beat the Colorado Rockies in four straight games to win its seventh World Series in franchise history. Ortiz had five hits and four RBIs in the four-game sweep, and Mike Lowell was named World Series MVP.

Three Titles and Counting

O ver the next few seasons, the Red Sox went through a number of changes. Ortiz's friend Manny Ramirez was traded to the Los Angeles Dodgers in 2008. The Red Sox traded for star first baseman Adrian Gonzalez in 2010 but later traded Gonzalez to the Dodgers two years later along with Josh Beckett and outfielder Carl Crawford.

Once merely the clubhouse clown, Ortiz had grown into a goofy yet respected member of the Red Sox roster. He hit twenty-three home runs and eighty-nine RBIs in 2008, and the Red Sox made it back to the ALCS before losing in seven games to the Tampa Bay Rays. In 2009, Ortiz hit twenty-eight home runs and ninety-nine RBIs but missed the All-Star Game

QUICK FACT

In 2009, the *Sporting News* named Ortiz the designated hitter of the decade. The Red Sox were also named the team of the decade.

AT BAT   BALL   STRIKE   OUT   H   E

Ortiz has grown into a fan favorite around the league because of his big hits and even bigger smile. Even fans of other teams like watching Big Papi play.

for the first time since 2003, as the Red Sox were swept by the Angels in the ALDS.

Ortiz and the Sox struggled in 2010, as Boston missed the play-offs for the first time since 2006 while Big Papi hit below the

Ortiz has become a popular figure in the annual Home Run Derby, which happens each year at the MLB All-Star Game. Big Papi often brings his son and two daughters on field to watch the festivities.

QUICK FACT

Ortiz won the 2010 All-Star Game Home Run Derby.

Mendoza Line in the season's early months. Many people expected the Red Sox to release Ortiz, as the Twins did back in 2002, but the slugger turned his season around and hit .270, with thirty-two home runs and 101 RBIs in 145 games.

As the Red Sox continued to miss the play-offs, Ortiz's numbers kept declining. Big Papi hit twenty-nine home runs and ninety-six RBIs in 2011 and played just ninety games in 2012, hitting twenty-three homers and sixty RBIs. Many thought again that Ortiz, at the age of thirty-six, was nearing the end of his career. Although Ortiz won his fifth Silver Slugger award in 2011 and made his eighth All-Star Game in 2012, the Red Sox continued to disappoint, missing the play-offs for the third straight season.

Clutch Once Again

QUICK FACT

In 2013, Ortiz set the record for career hits as a designated hitter, passing Harold Baines's previous mark of 1,688.

The 2013 season was a surprising one for both the Red Sox and Big Papi. Little was expected out of Boston, but Ortiz and the Sox surprised everyone by going from worst to first, winning the

In 2014, Ortiz presented President Barack Obama with a Red Sox jersey during a visit to the White House to celebrate the Red Sox's third World Series championship in less than a decade.

Big Papi does a variety of charity work helping children both in the United States and in his home country of the Dominican Republic.

AL East Division on their way to a third World Series title in a decade. Ortiz hit thirty home runs and 103 RBIs in the regular season, but it was his play-off performances that wowed fans once again.

Ortiz hit two home runs off Tampa Bay ace David Price in game 2 of the ALDS, which Boston won in four games. Boston struggled to score early in the ALCS against the Detroit Tigers, getting just one hit against Aníbal Sánchez in game one, but Ortiz turned the tide in game two. With Boston trailing 5–1 in the eighth, Ortiz smashed a grand slam into the Red Sox bullpen in Fenway Park, tying the game at 5. Boston won the game in the bottom of the ninth and the Red Sox bats woke up after that. Boston went on to win the series in six games to reach the World Series. Ortiz had only two hits in the ALCS, but his grand slam is one of the most memorable play-off home runs in Red Sox history.

Big Papi carried that clutch play into the "Fall Classic" against the St. Louis Cardinals. Ortiz homered in the first two games of the series, including an 8–1 game one win. Ortiz had eleven hits in sixteen at bats in the six-game series, driving in six RBIs and walking eight times. Boston won the series, 4–2, and Ortiz was named World Series MVP. The only member of all three World Series winning Red Sox teams of the last decade, Ortiz once again showed why he is considered one of the elite postseason hitters in baseball history.

Off-Field Papi

No man lives for baseball alone, not even David Ortiz. Ortiz met his wife, Tiffany, when he was playing A baseball in Wisconsin. When the team made the play-offs and the lease was up on his apartment, he moved into Tiffany's mother's house in Appleton, Wisconsin, until the season

QUICK FACT

Ortiz officially became a United States citizen on June 11, 2008, with a group of 220 immigrants at the John F. Kennedy Presidential Library in Boston, Massachusetts.

AT BAT BALL STRIKE OUT (H) (E)

ended. Ortiz and Tiffany's mom got along great, though, and she made him feel at home in Wisconsin.

David and Tiffany were married in 2002 and have three children. Their two daughters are named Alexandria and Jessica, while their son is named D'Angelo, after Ortiz's mother, Angela. Ortiz and his family used to have a house in Wisconsin, but they sold the house and moved to New England when Ortiz signed with the Red Sox. Ortiz still has an apartment in Santo Domingo, where he spends time in the winter.

Every year he has a golf tournament in the Dominican Republic to benefit his charity, the David Ortiz Children's Fund, which helps young people in New England and the Dominican Republic get health care and the treatment they need to beat childhood diseases. Ortiz started his foundation after meeting children having heart surgery in the Dominican Republic.

In 2006, when Ortiz set the Red Sox single-season home run

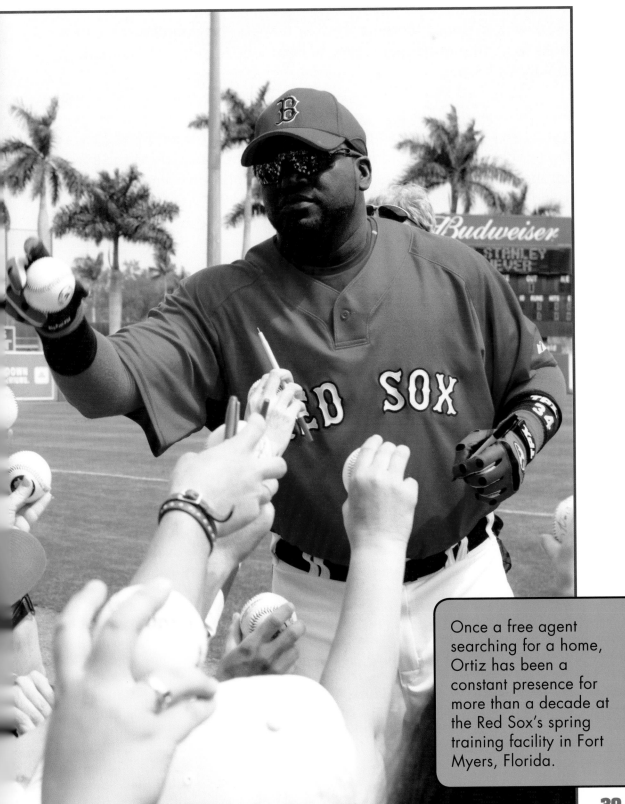

Once a free agent searching for a home, Ortiz has been a constant presence for more than a decade at the Red Sox's spring training facility in Fort Myers, Florida.

mark with a league-leading fifty-four homers, he donated some of the balls to charity to benefit Plaza de la Salud Hospital de Ninõs, a children's hospital in the Dominican Republic.

Many Red Sox players grew long beards during the 2013 season. Most started during spring training in February and grew them out all year. After they won the World Series, Ortiz and Red Sox centerfielder Shane Victorino each shaved their beards to raise money for the victims of the April 15 Boston Marathon bombings, which killed three people and injured more than 260. Ortiz continues to help children and others, including those affected by the bombings at the Boston Marathon in 2013.

1975   David Américo Ortiz Arias is born on November 18 in Santo Domingo, Dominican Republic.

1992   David Ortiz signs a major league contract with the Seattle Mariners on November 28.

1996   Ortiz is traded by Seattle to the Minnesota Twins on September 13.

1997   Ortiz makes his major league debut with the Twins and gets his first career major league hit, a double, against the Chicago Cubs on September 2. On September 14, Ortiz hits his first career major league home run against the Texas Rangers.

2002   Ortiz is released by the Twins on December 16.

2003   He signs with the Boston Red Sox on January 22; he hits thirty-one home runs and 101 RBIs in his first season with the team.

2004   Ortiz wins his first World Series with the Red Sox; he has his first All-Star appearance; and he wins his first Silver Slugger award.

2005   He drives in a career-high 148 RBIs with the Red Sox. He has his second All-Star appearance and wins his second Silver Slugger award.

2006   Ortiz hits the Red Sox-record of fifty-four home runs. He has his third All-Star appearance and wins his third Silver Slugger award.

2007 He wins his second World Series with the Red Sox; he leads the American League in on-base percentage. He has his fourth All-Star appearance and wins his fourth Silver Slugger award.

2008 Ortiz makes his fifth-straight All-Star Game appearance. On June 11, he becomes a U.S. citizen in Boston.

2010 Ortiz wins the All-Star Home Run Derby in his sixth appearance, on July 13.

2011 He makes his seventh All-Star Game appearance. He wins his fifth Silver Slugger award.

2012 Ortiz makes his eighth All-Star Game appearance.

2013 He wins his third World Series with the Red Sox and is named World Series MVP. He makes his fourth straight All-Star Game, ninth overall. He wins his sixth Silver Slugger award.

2014 Ortiz misses the final five games of the season because of a wrist injury. He will begin the 2015 season just thirty-four home runs short of the 500 mark in his career.

2015 Ortiz arrives at spring training injury free and ready to extend his major league record for most career hits by a designated hitter.

Randy Johnson (1963–) won his only World Series in 2001 with the Arizona Diamondbacks, also taking co-MVP honors. A five-time Cy Young award winner and ten-time All-Star, he won 303 games in his career and was inducted into the Baseball Hall of Fame in 2015.

Barry Bonds (1964–) is the all-time leader in home runs (762) and walks (2,558). He won seven National League MVP awards, including four straight from 2001–2004.

Greg Maddux (1966–) won four straight National League Cy Young awards, two with the Chicago Cubs and two with the Atlanta Braves. Maddux was inducted into the Baseball Hall of Fame in 2014. Winner of the Gold Glove eighteen times, he also won the 2005 World Series with Atlanta.

Curt Schilling (1966–) is a six-time MLB All-Star with 216 career wins. He won the World Series in 2001 with the Arizona Diamondbacks and in 2004 and 2007 with the Boston Red Sox. He was named World Series co-MVP in 2001.

Mariano Rivera (1969–) has the most saves (652) in MLB history. He won four World Series titles with the New York Yankees and was named World Series MVP in 1999. He was also named 2003 ALCS MVP, was a thirteen-time All-Star, and won the All-Star Game MVP in 2013.

Pedro Martinez (1971–) led the American League in earned run average (ERA) five times. He won a World Series with the

Red Sox in 2004 and was a three-time AL Cy Young award winner.

Manny Ramirez (1972–) won two World Series titles with the Boston Red Sox. This twelve-time All-Star had 555 home runs. He was World Series MVP in 2004.

Ichiro Suzuki (1973–) won both the MVP and Rookie of the Year awards in 2001 with the Seattle Mariners. He led the league in hits seven times, including 262 hits in 2004, the most all-time in a single season.

Derek Jeter (1974–) played twenty seasons and won five World Series with the New York Yankees. He is sixth all-time in hits. A fourteen-time All-Star selection, Jeter won Rookie of the Year in 1996 with New York.

Carlos Beltrán (1977–) was the 1999 Rookie of the Year with the Kansas City Royals. This eight-time All-Star has also won the Gold Glove three times.

Albert Pujols (1980–) won two World Series titles with the St. Louis Cardinals in 2006 and 2011. In 2001, he won Rookie of the Year. Pujols is a four-time National League MVP award winner and has more than 500 career home runs.

Tim Lincecum (1984–) has won two straight National League Cy Young awards in 2008 and 2009 with the San Francisco Giants. He is a four-time All-Star. He has thrown two no-hitters, in 2013 and 2014.

GLOSSARY

brink The edge at the top of a steep place.

curveball A baseball pitch that starts high and dips down past a hitter.

designated hitter A baseball player who does not play defense and bats instead of a fielding player, usually the pitcher.

disaster A sudden great misfortune.

double play A play in which the team in the field causes two runners to be put out.

elimination To be knocked out of the play-offs.

elite A successful and powerful person.

grand slam A home run hit with runners on all three bases, a four-run home run.

immigrant A person who comes to a country to live there.

lease An agreement to hand over real estate for a period of time, usually for a specified rent.

Mendoza Line A term describing a player with a batting average under .200, named after Mario Mendoza.

on-base percentage The percentage of at bats in which a baseball player safely reaches a base, or does not create an out.

rehabilitation The physical restoration of someone after an illness or injury.

routine A standard or regular way of doing something.

FOR MORE INFORMATION

Books

Freedman, Lew. *Boston Red Sox*. Edina, MN: ABDO Publishing, 2011.

Funk, Joe. *Baseball All-Stars*. Chicago, IL: Triumph Books, 2012.

Gilbert, Sara. *Boston Red Sox*. Mankato, MN: Creative Education, 2013.

Gonzalez, Tania Rodriguez. *David Ortiz*. Broomall, PA: Mason Crest, 2013.

Hammer, Max. *Superstars of the Boston Red Sox*. Mankato, MN: Amicus High Interest, 2015.

Hurley, Trish. *The 10 Greatest Comebacks in Sports*. Markham, CA: Scholastic, 2012.

Smithwick, John. *Meet David Ortiz: Baseball's Top Slugger*. New York, NY: PowerKids Press, 2007.

Stewart, Mark. *Clutch Performers*. New York, NY: Gareth Stevens Publishing, 2009.

Websites

Because of the changing nature of Internet links, Rosen Publishing has developed an online list of websites related to the subject of this book. This site is updated regularly. Please use this link to access the list:

http://www.rosenlinks.com/LLS/Ortiz

INDEX

THE NATIVE AMERICANS:
NAVAJOS

Text and Photographs by Richard Erdoes
Edited by Marvin L. Reiter

STERLING PUBLISHING CO., INC. NEW YORK
Oak Tree Press Co., Ltd.   London & Sydney

DEDICATION

*To my wife, Jean, whose patient help in any kind of
weather made this book possible.*

**This little Navajo girl is intrigued by a rodeo parade on one of her
rare visits to town.**

Photo Credits

Photos on pages 7, 12 and 13 courtesy of Smithsonian Institution, National
Anthropological Archives. Photo on page 44 courtesy of Larayne Parrish.

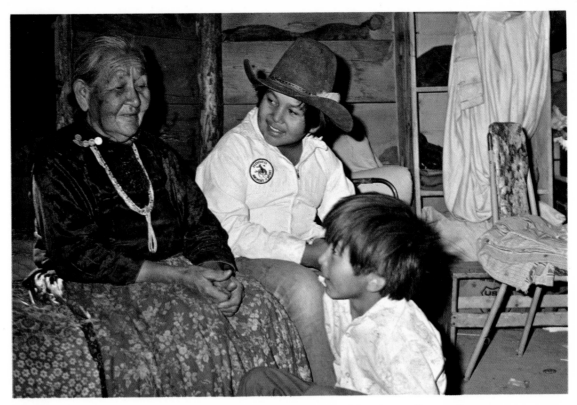

Grandparents play a big role in the life of Native American families. Telling their grandchildren the ancient tales and legends of the people, they fulfill a vital role as keepers of old traditions.

Contents

One of the best ways to experience the majesty of Navajo land is to sit at a table in the campground of Monument Valley Tribal Park, watching the sun rise or set over the Left Hand and Right Hand Mittens.

Part I: The History

To the Navajos the land in which they live is sacred. It was created by the Holy Ones for the people to live in. Men and animals had to pass through four previous worlds before emerging into this, the Fifth World of White Radiance. The Holy People put four sacred mountains at the corners of Navajo country and made it beautiful beyond words. They taught the people to live happily within this Land of White Brightness, in harmony with the earth, the streams, the plants and the animals. It is no wonder that the Navajos love this land, sacred to gods and men.

Who are the Navajos? Where did they come from? They call themselves "Dinneh"—the People. They did not always live in America's Southwest. Many tribes before them lived in what is now Navajo land. They were primitive hunters of huge, prehistoric beasts, woolly elephants and giant buffalos, basketmakers who lived in caves and the Anasazi—the ancient ones—who built cities against the walls of cliffs and on the flat tops of towering mesas.

Today the Navajos are a settled people. They are, in fact, the largest Indian tribe in the United States. But when they arrived in Arizona and New Mexico where they now live, they came as small groups of nomads, always on the move, bringing only what they could carry with them.

About the only solid fact we have in trying to reconstruct their past is their language, which is very similar to Athapascan, spoken by Canadian and Alaskan Indians living a thousand miles to the north of the Navajos.

It is generally believed that thousands of years ago all native American tribes drifted and trickled in small groups from Asia across the Bering Strait into Alaska. These people, who later were mistakenly called "Indians," were in reality Asians. Some crossed over the land bridge which many scientists believe once connected the two continents. Others walked across the mass of ice which covered the fog-shrouded Arctic waters during the Ice Age, following herds of mammoths and other big game ever southward towards the warming sun. These, then, were the people who became America's first immigrants.

Anthropologists are inclined to place the arrival of Navajos in the Southwest at anywhere between 800 and 1400 A.D. There appears to have been one great burst of immigration, followed by a succession of spurts and trickles extending over many generations.

Mystery shrouds much of their past. Are their hogans outsized copies of the wickiups, huts made from supple willow wands covered with skins, typical of many of the tribes in the Northwest? Why do these people, who once lived along coastal waters, now have a taboo against eating fish? Why are there no Athapascan-speaking people in the immense stretch of land between the Canadian Northwest and the Southwest of the United States?

At any rate, they arrived as small groups of hunters—men, women and children clad in the skins of animals. Later, these nomadic Indians split up into two related groups—the Navajos and the Apaches. The Apaches tended to be the more warlike of the two.

The newcomers were a hardy and resourceful breed. At that time they had neither horses nor cattle. Their only domestic animal was the dog—an animal that had attached itself to man thousands of years before. The early Navajos had no metal. Their weapons and tools were made of wood and stone. The men hunted while the women and children looked for edible bulbs, and nuts or berries. With their own hands they made whatever they needed—their weapons, their clothes, their huts.

The Navajos came out of the snowbound Northwest to the area in which they now live. Many Indian tribes from the Northwest and Canada belong to the same Athapascan language group as do Navajos. Modern Navajos are still surprised when they discover that they can understand many basic words of these people. Over a thousand years ago their northern relatives hunted buffalo on snowshoes. Northern Athapascans call themselves "Deneh" – the people – which is the same as the Navajo word for themselves – "Dinneh."

In this photograph, taken around 1880, an elderly man seems to think about the long-gone days of his youth when Navajo country was still part of Mexico and when many of his people had never seen a white man. Behind him, on the wall, hangs a blanket made of bobcat skins. He has blankets to wrap himself in, if the weather should turn cold. At that time the Navajos were just beginning to weave rugs instead of the old-style striped blankets. Early tourists, coming with the newly built railroads, had no use for wrap-around blankets but liked to decorate their homes with these colorful rugs.

Proud warriors, they also raided the granaries of the Pueblo villagers, who had learned to plant, reap and store corn and squash. The raiders also carried off Pueblo women. Becoming wives and mothers in their new homes, the Pueblos taught the Navajos many useful things, including the art of weaving.

The Navajos were, and still are, highly inventive people. Typical of their ingenuity was the sinew-backed bow which they brought to the Southwest. This weapon had greater force and accuracy than existing bows and helped them to improve their hunting prowess. Later on, they developed a rawhide moccasin boot, reaching halfway to the knee—providing good protection for their legs in the thorny chaparral country.

The Spaniards were the first white men to come into contact with the Navajos. Coronado was the first of several leaders of Spanish expeditions to penetrate the Southwest. In 1540 he came looking for gold. When he found none, he returned to Mexico. One of his lieutenants led a party of soldiers into Hopi country and probably also ran across some Navajos. In 1598

Navajos often fought against other tribes, such as the Utes of Colorado. The few early pictures of such encounters are seldom accurate when it comes to the costumes and weapons which were worn by the tribes at the time. This drawing is no exception.

Onate, another Spanish captain, arrived with a large expedition. He definitely encountered Navajo tribesmen. Unlike Coronado, Onate's expedition contained a number of settlers with their families and herds of cattle, sheep, goats and pigs. Onate became the first governor of the newly discovered, huge territory called New Mexico. The white men had come to stay. The name Navajo first appeared in the manuscript of a Franciscan friar in 1626. He had asked some Pueblo Indians what the name of the Dinneh people was. They said Navahu—which meant "planters of huge fields" in their language—and so Navajos they became, as far as the whites were concerned.

Why had they changed from nomadic warriors and hunters to settled planters? One explanation might be that with a rising population the game on which they fed had become scarce and they had no choice but to plant corn if they were to survive.

Possibly they already knew how to live by planting corn and other vegetables; how to weave baskets and make clay pots to carry their belongings on the trail when they first came to the Southwest. But it is more likely that they learned these things from the Pueblos who had been practicing these crafts for centuries. It appears that the Navajos had only to be exposed to anything new and they would turn it immediately to their practical benefit.

The picture shows how the traditional Navajo costume, as we know it today, began to evolve. The woman wears a blanket, a full, Spanish-style skirt and typical, knee-high moccasins. The man at the left wears the same hair style still in use among some traditional Navajos, but already has a white man's shirt. The Navajo warrior in the middle wears a Concho belt which is popular today and very expensive, but he is still armed with lance and bow.

The story continued the same with each new contact. From the Navajos' first encounter with the Spaniards they saw the value of cattle and horses—especially horses, which were to prove so useful to them in travelling over the vast distances of the Southwest. By trading, raiding and stealing, they lost no time in beginning to build herds of their own.

From the Spaniards they also learned the value of raising sheep—not only for food, but as a source of wool for weaving. This discovery was to point the tribe in an entirely new direction and to have an impact that would be felt in generations yet to come. By the close of the 18th century, Navajo weaving had not only become an important factor in the Navajo economy, but in the economy of the Spanish provinces—New Mexico, Sonora and Chihuahua—as well. Beautifully designed Navajo blankets and ponchos were in great demand during that period, and still are today.

Navajo history over the last two hundred years has been marked by tragedy. The Navajos were accustomed to hunting and raiding. The white men— first the Spaniards and Mexicans, then the "Anglos" or North Americans— greedy for Indian land kept trying to confine the native tribes in an

Massacre Cave, as depicted on a mural at Navajo Community College. In November, 1805, a large party of Spanish soldiers managed to ride into a branch of Canyon de Chelly. Many Navajo families, trying to escape the Spaniards' guns, took refuge in a cave high up in the canyon walls. The Spaniards, therefore, fired into the cave at random so that their bullets ricocheted from the walls and killed the people trying to hide inside. The Spaniards did not stop firing until all life in the cave was extinguished.

ever-shrinking space. The whites wore steel armor, had guns that spit fire, and finally, cannon. The end was never in doubt.

For the first few hundred years after their arrival in the Southwest the Navajos lived happily in their new land, spread out, undisturbed, over a vast expanse of desert. All this changed with the arrival of the white man. The Spaniards raided Indian settlements and carried off women and children as slaves. The Navajos in turn raided the Spaniards, partly to get back their loved ones, partly to add to their stock of horses and sheep.

Raiding became a way of life on the frontier. Indian tribes raided one another, and all raided Spaniards and Mexicans. The Apaches, because they were bolder and more ruthless at raiding, gave all the tribes a fearsome name. The Spaniards made a number of punitive expeditions into Navajo land in the 18th and the early years of the 19th century. On one occasion they trapped a group of Navajos in the Canyon del Muerte—"Death Canyon." Having no firearms to resist the Spaniards, about 200 Navajos took refuge in a large cave halfway up the sheer canyon walls. The Spaniards shot into the cave's mouth, hitting the walls and roof. The ricocheting bullets killed the

Indians, one by one, including women and children, until not a single Navajo was left alive. Cruelties inflicted by white men were often worse than anything the Indians did, but are generally not written about by white historians.

In 1848, after winning a war against Mexico, the United States took control of the Southwest and white North Americans began to move in. The raids and counter-raids continued. The whites formed vigilante mobs to deal with the Indians. Unable to make any headway, the Indians appealed to the government in Washington.

In April, 1862, Kit Carson, already famous as an Indian scout, was sent to put an end to the raiding, which meant the end of the old Indian way of life, once and for all.

Calling the Navajo leaders together, Carson told them that they must surrender to him. If they refused, he was ordered to wipe them out as a nation.

The Navajos decided to fight for their freedom. They made their last stand in the 1,000-foot-deep, rugged and forbidding Canyon de Chelly (pronounced *Shay*). Carson saw that he could not defeat them in their stronghold of steep red sandstone cliffs. So he decided on a scorched earth policy, destroying Navajo cornfields, cutting down fruit trees in their orchards, burning their

In 1847 the United States fought and won a war against Mexico. As a result the United States acquired a huge territory, usually referred to as the American Southwest, and the Navajo people came under American rule. Today, this area includes the states of Arizona, New Mexico, Utah, Nevada and California. (This colored lithograph, depicting the battle of Buena Vista in the Mexican War, comes from the Yale collection.)

This is Manuelito Segundo, son of the first Manuelito who was one of the greatest of Navajo chiefs. Young Manuelito went to Washington, D.C. as a member of a Navajo delegation in 1874. He is wearing the traditional Navajo costume of that time. The silver buttons in a row on the outside of his pants were copied from the Mexican caballero's costume. Manuelito is shown still armed with bow and arrow.

A photographer in 1892 still found a Navajo warrior dressed in pre-Spanish costume — a shirt of rawhide, a cap made of mountain lion skin with the ears still visible, a shield made of different layers of hide glued together, probably strong enough to turn not only an enemy arrow, but also an old-fashioned musket ball. He also wears the typical knee-high Navajo moccasins and still carries a long lance, a warrior's chief weapon until the coming of the "Anglos" of the North.

13

homes and driving off their herds of sheep and horses. Hunger finally forced the Navajos to surrender.

Kit Carson proceeded to round them up and drove them to his outpost at Fort Defiance. From there some 7,000 Navajos—men, women and children—were marched to a blistering hellhole called Bosque Redondo 300 miles away. The Navajo suffering on that march was exceeded only by the suffering of the Cherokee on their long trek from Georgia to Oklahoma, infamous as the "Trail of Tears." The old, the sick and the infirm were among those who set out along with the women, children and warriors. There were few wagons or horses. The old and the ill dropped out to die by the wayside. This tragic episode in Navajo history is still remembered with bitterness as "The Long Walk."

Those who were able to survive the journey to Bosque Redondo arrived to find no arrangements had been made to receive them. Lacking even the most miserable shanties, they were forced to dig holes in the ground like prairie dogs for shelter.

The poor soil, the terrible climate, the lack of planning, made even bare subsistence almost impossible. Summers passed, marked by one crop failure after the other. Even Washington began to realize that this was no solution to the Navajo problem. Meanwhile the ranks of the Indians grew thinner as every month more of them got ill and died under these brutal conditions. In July, 1867, one of the Navajo spokesmen told a United States commissioner:

"I am thinking all the time of my old country, hoping that the government will put us back there. We have worked here in heat and cold, and to no avail. What more can we do, what does the government want to do with us?"

In May, 1868, General William Sherman visited Bosque Redondo. He tried to persuade the Navajos to settle in the Indian Territory in Oklahoma, but they stubbornly refused to go there. Speaking for the whole tribe the Headman Barboncito asked that his people be allowed to return to their "beloved Red Rock Country":

"Our grandfathers had no thought of living in any other country than our own and it is not right we should abandon it. Here we plant, but the soil does not yield. All our animals have died. We have nothing left in the way of possessions but a gunnysack to wear during the day and to cover us at night. It makes my mouth dry and my head hangs low seeing us die here."

And so the United States finally concluded a treaty with the Navajos allowing them to return to their beloved ancestral home. Under the terms of the treaty the Navajos would receive some three million acres of desert land in northern New Mexico and Arizona which nobody wanted. The government also promised them a small sum for farm implements, 15,000 sheep and 500 head of cattle and, furthermore, a school for every 300 children. At dawn of the fifteenth day of June, 1868, the Navajos started on their long trek home—a ten-mile-long column of 7,304 Navajos with 1,500 mules and horses and 2,000 sheep and goats, surrounded on all sides by soldiers on horseback.

This picture shows the Navajos being driven out of their homeland to the desert wastes of Bosque Redondo, 300 miles away. Their homes and crops had been burned, their livestock slaughtered or stolen, and many of their loved ones killed. The pitiful group of survivors, most of them suffering from hunger and disease, had to walk on foot into captivity and many died along the way. This sad march is still talked about with great bitterness among Navajos, who remember it as "The Long Walk."

It took them five weeks to get back to their homeland, but this time they didn't mind the hardships of the trail. Again Barboncito spoke for all of them when he movingly and beautifully said:

"After we get back to our country, it will brighten up again, and the Navajo will be as happy as the land. Black clouds will lift and there will be plenty of rain to make the corn grow. It will grow in abundance and we shall be happy."

Finally, after years of anguish and incredible suffering, they returned to their beloved land. And they are still there today.

Navajo land is a big country, a land of brilliant colors, purples and blues, pinks and reds, yellows and greens, browns and grays. One large area, shown here, is a deep and uniform red. It is aptly known as "Red Rock."

Part II: The Land

"I see the Earth
I am looking at Her and smile
Because She makes me happy.
The Earth, looking back at me
is smiling too.
May I walk happily
And lightly
On Her."

The Navajo reservation—some 13 million-odd acres—is the largest Indian reservation of them all. It also has the largest membership of any tribe—an estimated 125,000. But in relation to the vastness of the land, they are hardly a drop in the bucket.

Wherever one may look, there are some of the most awesome spectacles of nature to be found anywhere, reducing man and all his proud works to nothingness. Here are contorted rock formations; strange mesas, or table lands; miles of parched desert, ending in walls of towering mountains. Even the air is not like other air; it is tangy with the scents of juniper, mimosa or sage.

It must be one of the least congested areas left on earth, for even the Navajos who live here, unlike other Indians of the Southwest, do not fancy living in villages or settlements. The hogan, their traditional dwelling, the one-family house is their limit so far as community participation goes (although their "family" may be extended to include more distant blood relatives up to the number of thirty or so). And the farther their hogan is from anyone else's hogan, the better.

This is Navajo land, the fabled "four corners," embracing large chunks of the northern parts of Arizona and New Mexico and little pieces each of Utah and Colorado.

It is a long way to anywhere in Navajo land, and a long, long way to Window Rock where the tribal offices are.

If it is 13 million acres of emptiness and sheep dip, it is also 13 million acres of breathtaking beauty, of sights not to be seen elsewhere. Within its confines

17

Strange rock formations rise abruptly out of the arid prairie. This one is just east of the town of Kayenta and has the look of an eerie moonscape.

are the unbelievable red formations of Monument Valley; the thirty-mile-long Y-shaped double gorge, the Canyon de Chelly. The Canyon is 500 feet deep and at its bottom is a world of its own. In Navajo land, too, are the Grand Canyon and the Painted Desert in all their glory.

There are strange things to be found here: primitive paintings, scratched into the walls of caves, some of the first efforts at artistic expression of early man; petrified dinosaur tracks; fossil remains of long-vanished bizarre creatures of overwhelming dimension; whole apartment complexes carved out of the walls of vertical cliffs and left abandoned, standing empty for centuries. Why? There are no answers. And fragments of artifacts give only tantalizing clues to a way of life no longer visible.

Although from a distance it might seem so, this is far from a barren land. The desert is rich with sagebrush, and a great variety of cactus. Farther up are the juniper bushes and piñon trees and higher up on the mountains, thick forests of cedar and yellow pines.

It throbs, too, with animal life of all kinds: the reptiles, from rattlesnakes to lizards of every kind, including the iguana and the deadly creature known properly as the Gila monster; the small scuttling creatures, the Kaibab squirrel and the black-tailed jack rabbit; and a small pig called the peccary.

Birds of prey ceaselessly glide over the forbidding desert lands looking for a mouse, a rabbit, a snake, or even a baby lamb.

For most of the year, the sky, arching over all, is a dependable turquoise blue; but the earth beneath is usually parched. A white man needs all his gadgets to help him survive here, such as a reliable car that will not break down in the heat in the middle of nowhere. But an Indian can survive because he knows. He knows which plants can be coaxed to give up their moisture to quench his thirst.

Then, when the moisture does come, it comes with a rush in the form of a cloudburst or a downpour. The earth returns its thanks and what had been a dry and dusty expanse bursts forth in rainbows of color.

To the Navajos, this land is not only theirs, it is sacred. It is their belief that

Horses grazing near the famous "El Capitan" rock formation make an unforgettable picture.

19

Monument Valley is known to all movie-goers as the site of many spectacular Western films. Among its formations are the Left Hand and the Right Hand Mittens. You can easily see how they got their names.

they did not come from elsewhere; they have always been here. According to their belief they evolved with the world from the time when the world was young and dark. The second world, or development stage, was blue; the third yellow, the fourth white.

They then emerged into the world they now see about them, the world of deserts, valleys, mesas, canyons and high mountains. The Holy Ones, they will say, brought us here.

Proudly, they will point out the sacred mountains marking the boundaries of their land, each of a color that corresponds to a stage in their development: to the east, the mountain of white shell (Mt. Blanca, Colorado); to the south the mountain of blue turquoise (Mt. Taylor); to the west, the mountain of yellow abalone (San Francisco Mountain near Flagstaff, Arizona); and to the north, the mountain of jet black (Mt. Hesperus, La Plata Mountains, Colorado).

The Fifth World, they say, is held up by these four pillars made of white shells, yellow abalone shells, blue turquoise and black jet.

This Fifth World of White Brightness is beautiful, but it, too, could be destroyed if the people living on it are not wise enough to live in harmony with it.

Thus not only is the land sacred to the Navajos but also all things both inanimate and animate living upon it. All these plants and animals have adapted miraculously to their environment. It is a tribute to the Navajo that he was able to do likewise—and a tribute to the land's strange beauty that it inspired people to adjust their lives to unbelievably harsh surroundings and find ways to support themselves in spite of the barren soil.

20

These needle-like rocks inside Monument Valley Tribal Park are known as the "Three Sisters."

This group of strange, pencil-shaped rocks within Monument Valley is known as the "Totem Poles." Monument Valley lies at the extreme northern end of the Navajo reservation, part of it extending into southern Utah.

The Navajo capital and administrative center gets its name Window Rock from this gigantic opening in a cliff overlooking the town.

On the top of this massive rock within Canyon de Chelly a group of Navajo warriors with their families made their last stand against soldiers led by Kit Carson.

Everywhere you look in Monument Valley, you see fantastically shaped formations surrounded by sagebrush, juniper and piñon trees.

At its western end, the Navajo reservation borders Grand Canyon National Park. This is a forbidding area with a stark beauty of its own, a barren land of multi-colored boulders and striped canyon walls.

24

West of Kayenta lies an area of solid, reddish sandstone. Though arid, this is still good sheep country. The area is dotted with secret caves, used by the ancient Indians for shelter and as hiding places from their enemies. Long before the arrival of the Navajos, their present homeland was inhabited by the prehistoric basketmakers and Pueblos to whom the Navajos gave the name of Anasazi – the "old ones."

Throughout Canyon de Chelly one can see many old Anasazi villages such as this one, known as White House Ruin. It consists of two parts – a lower apartment house complex on the valley bottom, and a small cliff town fairly high up in the wall which can be reached only by fearless climbers. The White House Ruin was inhabited from 1060 to 1275 A.D.

One of the most spectacular prehistoric ruins within the Navajo reservation is Betatakin, part of Navajo National Monument, about thirty miles west of Kayenta. Betatakin is a whole town nestling inside, and dwarfed by, a gigantic cave rising to a height of 600 feet above it. Cliff towns such as Betatakin were all abandoned before the end of the 13th century, mainly through lack of water, but also because the peaceful, corn-planting Anasazi had to make room for fierce raiding nomadic tribes moving into their territory.

This is a pictograph – figures painted on a rock wall in Canyon de Chelly by early Navajos with red, white and yellow earth colors. The figures probably represent masked and painted dancers.

Throughout Navajo land one finds many prehistoric rock paintings on the red sandstone walls. This one was made by the ancient Anasazi. It was probably not made for art's sake, but as a sort of hunting magic. By making an image of an antelope or mountain sheep the hunter sought to obtain power over it. These animal figures are in Monument Valley. They are "petroglyphs" – that is they are chipped out of the rock which is dark on the surface and bright red below the outer layer.

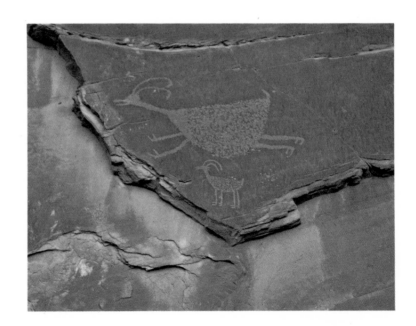

Throughout much of the 19th century the Southwest was described as the "Great American Desert." Its potential when irrigated, and its hidden treasures were then not even guessed at. Army officers who explored the region said it was fit "only for wild beasts and equally wild natives." Yet the desert is beautiful. In some places of the Navajo reservation there are areas of sand dunes. Those depicted here lie between the town of Chinle and Canyon de Chelly. Ripples in the sand caused by the ever-prevailing winds make beautiful patterns highlighted by the setting sun. Forbidding as the desert looks, the ancient Pueblos managed to grow their corn right out of sand dunes such as these.

Water is the lifeblood of Southwestern Indians. The arid desert blooms wherever it can be irrigated. But much of the area's water is diverted to the big cities of the whites. Winning the fight for their water is a matter of survival for the Navajos and the other tribes of Arizona and New Mexico.

The beauty and grandeur of the land cannot hide the fact that during much of the year the river beds are dry. "A mile wide and an inch deep" is how early travelers described the rivers of the Southwest, but often there is not even that one inch of water left.

In the heat of summer the rivers dry up under the rays of a pitiless sun and the river beds crack apart into fantastic patterns. As one young Navajo put it: "The earth has got a sunburn and its skin is peeling."

Everywhere the melting snows of early spring form little streams and rivulets. This is a good time for the people and their herds of sheep and horses.

All through the year sudden and unpredictable flash floods carry with them many thousand acres of desert earth, coloring the waters a deep, soupy red.

The passing seasons have their own color schemes. Spring brings forth ribbons of delicate green at the bottom of Canyon de Chelly's cliffs.

Summer heat turns Monument Valley into a landscape of pale ochre. Clouds promise rain, but do not always keep their promise.

Fall turns Dinetaa – the land of the Navajos – a deep, glowing yellow which, toward evening, is transformed by sun rays into glistening gold.

Far inside Canyon de Chelly rises Spider Rock, according to legend the home of a supernatural being called Spider Woman. Winter brings a sprinkling of snow. It seems that at that time of the year the light carries more ultra-violet, giving the landscape a purplish hue.

The immensity of the Navajo landscape reduces men and animals to mere specks, hardly noticeable unless their movements catch the eye.

The Navajo reservation has about a dozen major highways which connect the main Navajo towns to each other, as well as to the larger white cities surrounding the reservation. They give the tourist easy access to such natural wonders as Monument Valley, Canyon de Chelly, Grand Canyon, the Petrified Forest and the Painted Desert. They enable the strip-mining companies to get their coal out in oversized, rumbling trucks. But the majority of traditional people have to reach their hogans in the back country by way of unpaved trails, which seem to lead nowhere and which turn into mud whenever the weather turns bad.

It is no wonder that to the Navajo his land is sacred, the creation and abode of gods. Wherever you are in its wide expanse, you will find beauty and grandeur. "Beauty before me, and beauty behind me, beauty above me and beauty beneath me," according to the words of one Navajo chant.

Navajo country is Big Sky country. The sky is the abode of the Sun. According to Navajo legend, the Holy People travel on sunbeams, on the rainbow, on lightning. The clouds above, the earth below, the sun and the mountains together with all of nature are sacred to the Dinneh — to the people.

The Navajos are a nation of sheepherders. Wherever you go, you can see men and women, young or old, on horseback, driving their flocks to pasture.

Part III: The People: Traditional Life

The traditional Navajos live in houses called hogans. These are round huts with domed roofs, large enough to accommodate a family. Hogans are primitive dwellings, and usually have no windows or furniture, except a chair or two and a bed somewhere against the wall. They seldom have any modern conveniences such as electricity, running water or indoor plumbing. Water, which is very precious in this dry land, is usually hauled by wagon or pick-up truck from the nearest stream or spring.

Traditional Navajos like to have their hogans as far from those of other families as possible. Sometimes newlyweds, starting a home of their own, will build a smaller hogan not far from the home of the bride's mother. (It is perhaps a wise tenet of the tribe that one of the strictest of Navajo taboos is that a mother-in-law must never address her son-in-law directly but only through a third person.) Soon several smaller hogans may be clustered around the main hogan, like chicks around a mother hen. Navajo society is matrilineal, which means that not only the name but the money and all the property are handed down on the female side.

Here a man is herding his sheep to water them at a small stream west of Kayenta.

Almost all traditional Navajo homes, called hogans, have a sheep corral nearby. Mixed in with the sheep are often a number of Angora goats with huge, twisted horns. Their wool is highly prized by rug weavers.

Sheep are butchered near the hogan. Mutton, served with corn and fry bread, is the staple food of the people.

This old woman tends her flock on foot in Monument Valley. The two great rocks known as "mittens" make a picturesque background.

These families are also units in a larger social community; but not in any sense a community as we know it—a physical cluster of houses, stores and offices. It is a kind of basic communications center, perhaps only a crossroads on the desert where one might find a post office, a gas station or a trading post.

Young modern Navajos may work in an office or factory, on or near the reservation; but for the traditionals, sheepherding and weaving the wool into the much coveted rugs is still the main source of income. And a lucrative mainstay it is. A fine woven article, one which may have taken the weavers several months to complete, may bring anywhere from $1000 to $2500 or more.

Sheep raising is a more difficult enterprise in Navajo land. This is due to the short supply of good grazing land. Navajo shepherds are forced to move their flocks over great distances in order to provide the animals with enough grass to eat. For this reason these Navajo families maintain two or three hogans, located in widely scattered areas. They move from one hogan to another as soon as an area becomes "grazed out." The most traumatic shock that the Navajos had suffered since "The Long Walk" of the last century came in the 1930's, when the United States government declared the Navajos guilty of overgrazing, and decreed that the tribe slaughter half its sheep. It took a long time for the flocks to recover their former size.

In the past, the sheep were tended primarily by young Navajo children. Today, compulsory education demands that these children attend school, even those living in the most remotely located hogans. It is not unknown in these

39

Sheep are not only kept for their meat, they are mainly kept for their wool which is woven into the famous Navajo rugs. Before it can be used, the wool must be carded and spun into yarn. The carding is done between two small wooden boards with handles to get rid of impurities, such as burrs. The spinning is done with a simple, long-handled spindle which is twirled to make tufts of wool into a continuous thread. This simple process has been used all over the world for thousands of years.

parts for a school bus to travel forty miles to a distant hogan and forty miles back again just to get one child to school. The literacy rate has increased dramatically, but the families have been deprived of their supply of young shepherds. The job of herding the sheep has, therefore, fallen to adult members of the family, often the grandparents.

Navajo weaving is performed exclusively by the women of the tribe. One of the more miraculous aspects of tribal life is the sight of two women, seated in the yard outside the hogan, with fingers and wooden shuttles flying across the loom. They weave rugs with no preconceived pattern, never exchanging a word while creating designs that have become known throughout the world for their beauty and originality.

Here are two Navajo women before the traditional loom set up in front of the hogan. At the left, Elta Dee is carding the wool. The carder is made up of rows of nails set close together. The wool is combed through these nails until all the little sticks, burrs and stones imbedded in it have been removed. At the right, Susie Black does the actual weaving. Among the Navajos, rug weaving is always done by women.

The skilled weaver progresses quickly and soon the rug takes shape. Colors and patterns vary from district to district. Rug making has become important in the Navajo economy. A large, well-woven rug with an intricate pattern can sell for up to two or three thousand dollars. On the other hand, it might take months to finish. As the Navajos believe that nothing man-made should be perfect, a small mistake is always woven into the rug.

The high rewards of rug-making greatly enhance the importance of women in the scheme of things. Taking a rug all the way from a sheep's back to the outstretched hand of a prospective purchaser requires many decisions each step of the way. This is where the women, who do the weaving, have the chance to become experienced in deciding business matters. This attribute is easily broadened to include other matters relating to family affairs as well.

Navajo rugs are deserving of their reputation. They are durable and long-lasting, not only because of the experience of the weavers, but the care with which they are made. The wool is meticulously sorted and combed until all the burrs and twigs are removed. It is then washed in soap suds made from the yucca plant. It is carded between boards studded with many nails, then spun and respun on a long spindle, one end of which rests on the ground.

Native plants keep the weavers supplied with a rich arsenal of natural colors to be used for dyes, including yellow from the goldenrod, green from

Besides rug weaving, making jewelry is a craft for which the Navajos are famous. Silversmithing was introduced by the Spaniards and Mexicans around the middle of the 19th century. Metal was obtained from melted-down American silver dollars or Mexican pesos. Originally only men made silver jewelry, but nowadays, defying tradition, a few women also try their hand at it.

Small herds of cattle can also be found in Navajo land but, except in certain spots, it is really not very good cattle country. Here a herd is driven through Monument Valley.

42

And here is a close-up of two young Navajo cowboys.

The face of a young Navajo dancer reflects the intensity with which he moves as he is carried away by the rhythm of chant and drums on dance night.

sagebrush, orange from lichens, violet from holly berries, and dark brown from the piñon trees. Indigo is an exception. The Navajo weavers have purchased that dye from traders for hundreds of years.

When traditional women go to the trading post to market their wares or appear at tribal headquarters for other reasons, they almost invariably wear their knee-high moccasins of calfskin, their calico skirts, and their loose-flowing blouses of bright-colored velvet or velour. Over their heads is flung a bright kerchief. And they will very likely be wearing their hair in the prescribed Navajo knot at the back of the head.

The men are inclined to be tall and slim-waisted. Wearing pointed boots, blue jeans, dark shirts and ten-gallon hats, they might be taken for cowhands, except for the feather they wear in their hatbands, a reminder of their pride in being Indian.

Navajo men on first acquaintance are likely to appear aloof. Their reserve is one of shyness, however, and on closer acquaintance they become very friendly.

Wandering through the reservation, if lucky, you may see nailed to a tree or to a fence-post a hand-lettered sign which reads: "Dance Tonight," or "Sing Tonight."

You are invited. Everyone is invited. But not inside. You approach a hogan. From afar you hear the drums beating. In the light from the campfire you see a circle of shiny bronzed faces. They are laughing, shouting, singing along with the music. They are having a good time.

But you are not permitted to go inside the hogan.

There, seated on the floor, is a medicine man. The Navajo medicine man, who is also an artist, is busily at work fashioning a sand painting. He was not permitted to begin the painting until after the sun set. It must be destroyed before the sun comes up. (If he had started it during the daylight hours, he would have had to destroy it before sunset.) In the meantime, the sand painting will be the centerpiece in a curing ceremony. At a certain point the patient will be asked to go and sit in the middle of the sand painting so that the spirits may reach him directly through it, and thus help to speed his recovery. Outside—songs, dancing and merriment. Within, a man or woman who is very ill, hoping to ward off disease or death.

With the traditional Navajo, social life and religion cannot be separated. They form the very essence of their lives.

Treasured throughout the world, Navajo jewelry is made by a process called sand-casting. In this method hollow molds are carved from soft tufa stone and then molten silver is poured into them or, as the experts say, "cast." Besides silver, turquoise and, less often, coral are used in Navajo jewelry. Traditional native craftsmen use only genuine turquoise while non-Indian imitators often use fake turquoise made of colored plastic.

The sand painting is part of a "sing" which is the Navajo name for a great number of rituals. To have a "sing" it is necessary to procure the services of a particular type of medicine man called the Hatali—or chanter. He is one who brings evil under ritual control. He is the diviner diagnosing the cause of a sickness. His knowledge has not been acquired quickly. Before a "sing" he spends days in fasting, taking sweat baths, in lone vigils communing with the "powers." He searches for the cause of evil through "listening" or by looking at the stars, or by eating an herb of enlightenment, but most often by trembling. His whole body shakes, his trembling hands wander, hesitate, hover over a patch of cornmeal until finally the finger traces upon it some ancient design. It then indicates the cause of the disease and the appropriate ritual.

The sand painting is part of the chant, lasting from five to nine days during which a different painting is made each day. There are almost 500 different

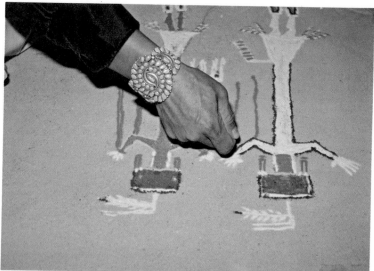

A Navajo medicine man is just starting to make a sand painting. Actually it is not made of sand at all, but of ground-up charcoal and minerals and it would be better to call it a "dry painting."

designs for sand paintings and almost as many chants. Some sand paintings are small and can be finished in an hour or two. Other special ones might be twenty feet long, requiring the help of a dozen assistants if it is to be completed within the specified time. When the ceremony is over, man and painting are symbolically and physically united. The medicine man dips his fingers first into a liquid and then into the sand painting, transferring some of the sand to the patient's skin, bringing him in tune with its symbolic meaning and giving him some of its power.

In these ceremonies, while the singing and the dancing are going on

Some sand paintings are small, about two feet wide, and can be made by one or two men in an hour. Others are up to twenty feet wide and take fifteen men a whole day to complete. There are hundreds of different designs generally depicting the legendary "Holy People." The medicine man will discuss with the patient or his family which design to use for the particular illness or problem. There are also many sacred chants to be sung during a ceremony – such as "Blessing Way" or "Beauty Way."

The Navajos' traditional home is the hogan, a structure of wood covered with mud, surprisingly warm in winter and cool in summer. This is a modern, six-sided hogan nestling within Canyon de Chelly.

outside, inside the hogan the patient's confidence is being restored as he listens to the words of the chant:

"Happily I recover
Happily my interior becomes cool
Happily my eyes regain their power
Happily my head becomes cool
Happily my legs regain their power
Happily I hear again!
Happily for me the spell is taken off!
Happily may I walk
In beauty I walk."

"Sings" are held not only to free a person from illness or an evil spell. Medicine men pray for rain or other natural phenomena, or for good fortune in practical affairs. They also conduct rituals to mark important events in the life of a family or an individual.

The aim of the Navajo at a quick glance seems simple enough. He wants merely to do the right thing, to go through life the right way, the "Singing Way." But if he is to follow traditional beliefs, he will find himself limited by taboos on every hand. He will avoid a tree struck by lightning, never kill a snake, or eat raw meat. Indoors, he will never step over a sleeping person or have any contact with his mother-in-law, and so on.

Today one rarely encounters the old-style hogan whose main support consisted of three forked sticks and had an extended entranceway. Somewhat off center was the smoke hole. Old-style as well as modern hogans always face the rising sun. If someone should die inside the hogan, his body must be taken out through a hole in the rear. Among very traditional Navajos, the hogan itself with everything in it is then abandoned.

47

Somewhere near each hogan stands the sweat lodge — a miniature hogan, its door facing east. Basically the sweat lodge is a sauna. In it men crouch to purify themselves. Hot, red-glowing rocks are brought into the lodge and cold water is sprinkled over them. The searing, hot steam rises, bathing the men's bodies, opening pores and minds. After the steam bath the men dry themselves with sand or, in wintertime, roll in the snow. Unlike the white man's sauna, the Indian's sweat lodge purifies the spirit as well as the body. The steam bath is, as a matter of fact, a religious ceremony. Sacred songs are sung during the bath and the "Holy People" are invited to come and join in.

This old woman lives all alone in a small hogan near Lukachukai with only her cat to keep her company. As with almost all hogans the stovepipe sticks out of the earthen roof.

But even the very small, isolated hogan can be snug and comfortable. Good meals are cooked on a simple wood stove. Traditional Navajos are not encumbered by the many possessions and gadgets which clutter up the homes of whites. They are essentially very poor by white standards, which are not always applicable on Indian reservations.

Some of the hogans are large and roomy, but the basic features are always the same—an earthen floor and an iron stove with the stove-pipe in the middle. Furnishings are meagre and life is hard. During the cold season, and when it rains, the weaving loom is set up inside the hogan.

White people often wonder how the many members of a typical Navajo family can live, eat, sleep and store their possessions in a one-room hogan no more than twenty feet across. People who live that close to each other with little privacy have learned to treat each other with respect and consideration. Old customs of how to behave inside the hogan are a great help. Women always sit on the north side of the hogan, men on the south. The smaller children stay close to their mother. The place of honor is on the west side facing the door. Possessions are stacked in trunks and boxes against the walls. Everything has its place. Many objects are hung from nails in the roof beams. Wood and kitchen utensils are placed near the stove.

Some modern hogans are more or less equipped like the homes of white people. Though most of them lack electric light or running water, they can be cozy and comfortable. This is Susie Black's hogan in Monument Valley.

The traditionals are also beset with fears. They fear the Holy People. These are mysterious supernatural beings who exercise strange power over the destinies of the living. They try through various rituals to satisfy the Holy People and win their support. Even more fearsome are the Witches. But the worst fears of all are reserved for the dead. This is so extreme that once a person has died in the hogan a hole must be cut in the wall for the body to be carried out. Then the hogan, with all its contents, is quickly abandoned.

But in spite of all these taboos and fears the Navajos seem to derive enough spiritual support from their "sings" and ceremonies to make their way through life as smoothly as possible.

From the time of birth, the Navajo child's progress through life is marked by rituals. Long after the introduction of the white man's iron, Navajos still used a flint to cut the umbilical cord.

The woman who assists in the birth has the privilege of bathing the newborn child. The baby is then ritually placed at its mother's left side, lying with its head toward the north and the fire, to be anointed with corn pollen—a symbol of life.

A cradleboard which has been made for it by the father is ready and waiting. Here the baby will spend the first few months of its life. As the baby is being placed in it, a special song is chanted:

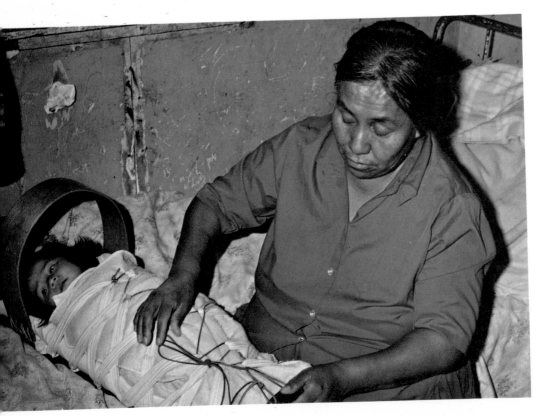

Among traditional families a baby spends much of its first year strapped and swaddled in a cradleboard. In one form or another, cradleboards were used in most Indian tribes. Cradleboards can be strapped to the mother's back while she is working; they can be tied to a saddle horn when travelling; they can be put upright against a tree or hogan wall, so that the baby can watch what is going on. Thus, cradleboards were perfectly adapted to the Indian way of life.

Watching over the baby and carrying it around is often a chore for an older sister. Children learn at an early age to take responsibilities and fit themselves into the rhythm of traditional life. The obvious practicality of Indian cradleboards has, in recent years, led to the manufacture of baby-carriers made in imitation of them, so that white mothers can tote their little ones around. A bent, circular wooden strap at the cradle's top protects the baby's head.

"I have made a baby board for you
   my son (daughter)
May you grow to a great old age
Of the sun's rays I have made the back
Of black clouds I have made the blanket
Of rainbow I have made the bow
Of sunbeams have I made the side loops
Of lightning have I made the lacings
Of sundogs have I made the footboard
Of dawn have I made the covering
Of black dog have I made the bed."

The baby is strapped to his mother's back, enabling her to take the child with her wherever she goes. At the same time, her hands and arms are free to do weaving, work in the garden or whatever daily chores are necessary.

When the child enters adulthood, a special ritual takes place.

Towards the end of this ritual, called the Yeibachi, two masked dancers with frightening faces are introduced to the children. When the dance is finished the dancers take off their masks and the children see they have been worn by relatives. Then they are permitted to put the masks on and look through them. In this way, they are relieved of their fears and made to feel grown up.

When it comes to finding a mate, the young Navajo faces only one rule: he or she may not marry within the clan or within the father's clan.

In the old days the young suitor used to come courting with a deer slung over his shoulder, proving that he was an accomplished hunter, and the girl could thus be assured that he was a good provider. Today he is more likely to come with a beautiful horse as a gift. If the young man's proposal is accepted, he will then move into the hogan of his bride's mother, or possibly her grandmother.

Soon the young couple will be able to move into a smaller hogan of their own nearby. This calls for another ritual, known as the "Blessing Way." Their new home will be anointed with corn pollen to assure the young couple's happiness.

In the years ahead, the young couple in times of trouble will seek the support of the Holy People "to keep their feet on the Blessing Way."

Old-fashioned Navajos are good and loving parents who seldom scold and never beat their children. The young ones are therefore happy and laugh a lot, but are a little shy when meeting strangers.

There are few toys in a traditional hogan and no television sets. Children are therefore resourceful in inventing their own games.

The area around the hogan makes a fine playground. It is fun to take little sister for a ride and to show off one's prize possession — a new, shiny bicycle.

While life inside a hogan has its charm, one should not romanticize it. Life is also hard without the conveniences even the poorest of white families are used to. Wood for fuel has to be chopped and often transported over great distances. Water has to be hauled. There are no gadgets to do the housewife's work for her. People are poorer, have a shorter life span and less medical care than their white fellow citizens. Amusements are few. As one young woman said: "It is beautiful, but also sad to live the Indian way."

Many tourists are surprised at having their cars serviced and tires fixed by pretty Navajo girls.

Part IV: The People: Modern Life

The Navajos have a special song—a happiness song. One can often hear some young people on horseback singing it over and over again as they are riding, side by side, through Canyon de Chelly, their voices echoing back and forth from the sparkling red canyon walls glowing in the warmth of the evening sun.

To the casual observer, the modern Navajo has every reason to be happy. He, or she, is handsome to begin with—Navajos are among the most graceful and beautiful people in the world. Modern Navajos often live in homes with many of the comforts usually found in a white, middle-class family. They certainly seem to have plenty of room to stretch in. Their reservation is, after all, bigger than two New England states put together. There is much natural beauty above ground and untold treasures below—coal, oil, natural gas, even uranium in some places. The exploitation of these natural resources means jobs for Navajo men and women. Wherever the land is irrigated, there are good crops. The forests of the high country yield valuable timber. At Window Rock, the Navajo capital, well-dressed Navajos and white businessmen can often be seen discussing deals. Young Navajo officials walk with an air of confidence. Public buildings are impressive. The Tribal Council building at Window Rock is designed like a great hogan. Its murals wonderfully depict Navajo history, and the councilmen conduct their business with the seriousness of the United States Senate. The Navajo Community College at Tsailie rises out of the mountain-rimmed desert—an enormous octagonal building visible for many miles, reflecting the rays of the sun and drifting clouds. The gigantic wood-processing machines at the tribal sawmill, and modern schools and hospitals give an impression of wealth and progress.

But, unfortunately, this picture is deceiving. A reader of the *Navajo Times* expressed the plight of the Native American living a white lifestyle:

"I have a job, good wages and house, a car, food on the table and plenty of clothes. Yet, there is something missing in my life. These things should be all that I and my family need, but somehow it is not enough.

"I live in a new housing development built on a mesa, where there was

George Holiday, Navajo guide and jeep tour leader, stands—a tiny figure—outlined against Monument Valley's majestic skyline.

only sand, rocks and sagebrush a few years back; but I don't know my neighbors. I hardly leave my house to look at the night sky or the sunlight or the sandstone cliffs.

"At night I watch television. My life and the lives of my children are as empty as the programs on television. We live from purchase to purchase—a new car, a new refrigerator, new clothes; material things which give us the momentary pleasure of new possessions and then leave us wondering what next new thing to look forward to.

"The children ride by bus for hours to go to a brand new school which sticks up from the top of a mesa; an enormous, multi-colored box which does not fit the beauty of high desert landscape.

"My children have hardly learned to read and write at the school. At night they do not read books. They watch television. What will they do to earn a living when they are grown? Will machines do their reading, writing and mathematics for them? If so, what functions will be left to occupy their minds and bodies?

"We become separated from our culture and forget the way things used to be. Our parents and those of their community are rooted in the land and everything they do and think is related to the land on which they live. We no longer feel this close connection, and so it is hard for us to understand them and feel the things they feel, just as it is hard for them to know how it is with us. When we return home we no longer feel comfortable in the hogan. It is uncomfortable for us. We are used to running water and supermarket foods, more separation from the weather, more personal privacy and all the other things to which one becomes accustomed in the technological society. When it comes time to leave, we are glad to return

58

The Navajo reservation has large deposits of surface coal. Coal companies are strip-mining these deposits at Black Mesa and elsewhere. Giant machines, called draglines, remove the topsoil to lay bare the coal beneath it. With each bite, the dragline's huge shovel scoops up chunks of earth the size of a small house.

Among the reservation's resources is natural gas, and exploration for it is underway.

Navajos are proud of their sawmill, one of the largest and most modern in the world. It is operated and staffed by the tribe.

59

Power lines criss-cross Navajo land. Some stretch for hundreds of miles, bringing electricity to distant cities. Coal mined on the reservation is shipped to huge power plants where it is converted into energy.

A coal chute several miles long conveys coal from the top of Black Mesa to a huge tower where it will be loaded on freight trains. This operation, which requires a great deal of water, is a source of concern to Navajos and environmentalists alike. Water is in short supply in Navajo land.

Strip-mining often results in great, perhaps permanent, damage to the environment. Some coal companies make great efforts to restore the landscape to its original shape and are proud of their filling and reseeding program which is supposed to result in more grazing land for the tribe.

to the comfort of our civilized home, to the emotional oblivion of television."

A young college student simply said: "It's hell to be an Indian and a white man at the same time. You are still not accepted among whites, and you can't relate to the old folks any more. You even forget your language. You belong nowhere."

In spite of natural resources and some signs of better living conditions at a few centers such as Window Rock, most Navajos live in abject poverty. Many families have an income of only fifty dollars a week.

Unemployment is officially estimated at 40 per cent and rises to 75 per cent in certain areas. Navajos, like other Indians, suffer from job discrimination and, when employed, often get jobs only at the lowest level, regardless of qualification. Ninety per cent of the families live in sub-standard houses, or hogans without plumbing, sometimes without electricity. Eighty per cent of the people must still haul their water by pick-up truck for distances of more than a mile. Shopping is not always easy and the trading post is often far away. The white trader in many cases has no competition for miles around and sets prices which are higher than those in New York, Chicago or Los Angeles. Many people, even educated Navajos working for the Federal Government, live in isolation. Bad weather makes the many dirt roads impassable. During severe weather conditions food has to be flown into some communities by helicopter.

Health care is also sub-standard. Navajos have a life span which is ten years less than the national average. The death rate from tuberculosis is eight times

61

greater than among whites. Infant mortality is high. The people still suffer from diseases which have long been eliminated in the rest of the country.

Schools have problems too. Teachers often do not speak both languages—Navajo and English—as they should. Only a handful of teachers are Indians. Teaching material does not always reflect Indian values and life as the Navajo child knows it. Caught between two cultures and faced with few prospects for jobs as adults, many Indian students drop out.

Poverty, cultural conflicts, and the resulting psychological pressures have caused alcoholism among many young people.

The tribe is now making a vigorous effort to combat alcoholism. In health clinics and tribal offices one sees posters showing that in all the Indian battles and massacres, from Sand Creek to the Custer Fight to Wounded Knee, fewer Indians were killed than were killed by alcohol. Among those who have been enlisted to treat alcoholism are traditional medicine men, who are said to have better success than many white doctors.

White tourists often wonder why there should be so much poverty, bad housing and bad health in a tribe with so much land and natural resources. The answers are easy to find. Most of the land is desert. It blooms only where it is irrigated and water is generally scarce. Much of this precious water, however, is often diverted by both State and Federal governments to serve the needs of whites.

Coal and oil resources did not make the individual Navajo rich. First of all,

Although industrialization is desirable to raise the living standard of the people, it seems always to be connected with a certain amount of pollution. As we can see here, air pollution is a growing problem.

The tribal council building at Window Rock is built in the shape of a traditional hogan. It is a beautiful building blending harmoniously into the Navajo landscape.

Inside the tribal council 74 council members representing various communities under the chairmanship of the tribal president vote on all matters of importance submitted to them. President and council members are elected by the democratic process—just as are congressmen and senators.

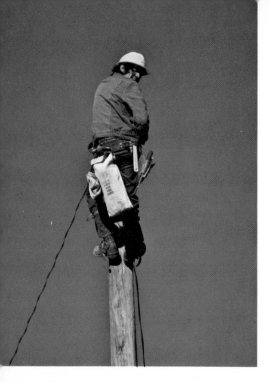

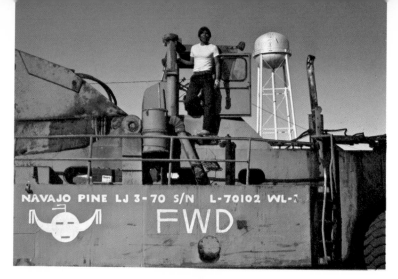

Giant trucks at the tribal sawmill carry huge tree trunks as if they were matchsticks. All heavy equipment at the sawmill is operated by Navajos. Native timber from the high forests in the northern part of the reservation furnishes the raw material.

Growing industrialization means job opportunities for many Navajos. In a land where there is high unemployment, this is of major importance. Here we see a telephone wireman at work, improving the communications system on the vast reservation.

Women have always played a very important role in Navajo life. They express self-assurance and confidence by taking on many jobs which elsewhere are usually performed by men.

Navajos are famous today for the ease with which they adapt to the technological age. They have a special aptitude for mechanics —whether operating heavy machinery, or working on miniature electronic equipment.

More and more college-educated Navajos repay the tribe for scholarships received by returning to work on the reservation as engineers, foresters, plant managers, accountants or doctors.

The sergeant is a lady! Navajos are proud of their tribal police force. The police academy at Window Rock graduates two dozen or so new officers every year, among them a number of women. The ladies of the force can rise to any position. Driving patrol cars and armed with a six-shooter, they mean business. Uniforms are handsome, more so than in much of the rest of the country.

Women make up a large part of the staff of the *Navajo Times,* which is published weekly at Window Rock.

Much technical work goes into the making of a newspaper. Here we see film being developed. The *Navajo Times* is a modern, concerned and highly professional paper, proud of its in-depth reporting and special issues on such subjects as federal politics, health and education, the practices of pawnshops and trading posts or tribal finances.

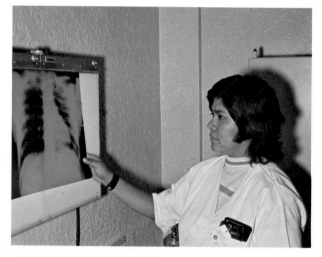

The Navajos have many health problems such as tuberculosis, trachoma (eye disease), and alcoholism. Patients are cared for in hospitals on and off the reservation where more and more registered nurses and skilled lab technicians on staff are Indians.

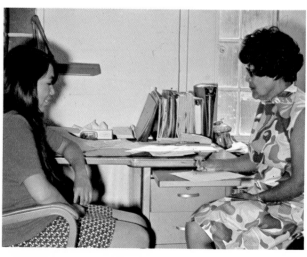

Patients with mental problems are frequently treated by native psychiatrists, who have a better chance of helping them because of their intimate knowledge of Navajo life.

there are too many Navajos to share this wealth. With a population of close to 150,000 the Navajos are the largest tribe in the United States. The land and the resources are simply not enough to feed everyone. Oil and coal companies negotiated treaties with the tribe for the exploitation of its natural resources. However, these treaties give the companies the major share of profits, leaving too little for the Indians from whose land these treasures are taken. Strip mining destroys large tracts of grazing land and uses up an enormous amount of already scarce water, while providing only an insignificant number of jobs for Indians. Industrial pollution is contaminating air, water, livestock, and crops.

The Navajo tribe has been likened to a nation within the nation—an underdeveloped, "third world" nation trying to catch up with the rest of the country.

Today's young Navajos are faced with all the problems of modern life which they share with their white fellow citizens. In addition, they have to cope with problems peculiar to their land, their tribe and their being Indians. They carry a double burden and they carry it well. As a group they have successfully withstood obliteration by the alien white culture. With their remarkable adaptability, they have been able to use this culture for their own needs without being completely overwhelmed by it. A typical symbol is the traditional medicine man driving his shiny brand-new pick-up truck. Navajos are mastering the present, while facing the future with courage and moral stamina.

New modern housing projects are springing up near all population centers.

The population explosion brings the need for instant housing. Trailer parks are common. This one stands amid red sandstone formations which give it its name: "Baby Rocks."

Many Navajo homes are isolated specks in an immense landscape, miles away from the nearest neighbor and frequently cut off by bad weather. Every year during snow storms or flash floods some hogans and small communities have to be supplied or rescued by helicopter.

In spite of fledgling industries and natural resources, the over-whelming majority of the people are still poor and unemployment is high. Poverty is reflected by slum housing. Many Navajos still live in shacks without modern conveniences.

Navajo children learn that they are expected to do their share of the housework, which may include helping to prepare the family meals.

Increasing numbers of young Navajo couples live in modern homes and cook with gas while their mothers still make do with the old wood-burning stoves inside their hogans.

Young couples keep up with the news with the *Navajo Times*. This young woman is studying the sales ads, her husband the tribal football results.

In modern Navajo homes, as everywhere else, high school students are busy with their homework.

Like all children, modern Navajo youngsters are great TV watchers, arguing loudly whether to turn on Mickey Mouse or Sesame Street.

Many people have for-
gotten what an old-
fashioned washboard
looks like. The Indians
have not. In isolated
areas, and in the absence
of electricity, a woman's
muscle power has to do
the job of a washing
machine.

Sometimes it is hard to
label a family "modern"
or "traditional." Alice
Johnson (at the left)
speaks almost no English
and spends most of her
time weaving Navajo
rugs. Her husband is a
National Park Ranger.
Sometimes they live in a
modern home provided
by the park service; at
other times they live in
an old-style hogan.

Arts and crafts play a big
role in the Navajo econ-
omy. This man makes
decorative sand paint-
ings. He first applies glue
to the design and then
sprinkles colored sand
over it. These sand paintings use many motifs
similar to the dry paint-
ings made for curing ceremonies, but are strictly
items to be traded to
whites and, of course, are
not sacred.

Navajos contribute more than their share of men to the armed forces. Navajos have fought in World Wars I and II, in Korea and in Vietnam. Navajo families proudly display photographs showing their men in uniform.

Flags fly from the graves of Navajo soldiers who gave their lives for America. During World War II many Navajos worked as radio-men since neither Germans nor Japanese listening in on their conversations could understand their tribal language.

Many trading posts are run by whites. Navajos complain that traders will no longer make loans on Indian jewelry and that prices are higher here than outside the reservation. As everywhere else, there are good traders and bad traders.

Many families travel miles to buy at the only trading post in their vicinity.

Old trading posts are often colorful. They are part of Navajo history. Traders were responsible for encouraging Navajos to weave rugs for the tourist trade and also, for many years, they were the only outlet for Navajo jewelry.

Hubbell's trading post, now a historic landmark and museum, still sells old-fashioned items popular among the hogan-dwelling people —saddles and horse blankets, cradle boards, colorful shawls, spindles for making wool yarn, huge Mexican-style spurs, broad-brimmed "Uncle Joe Hats," and bright sateens for ladies' skirts.

There are many bright, new schools everywhere. Navajo families are large and the number of students is steadily rising.

School buses stop at isolated road crossings, letting two or three children off at a time. Some children from sheepherding families travel 80 miles (128 km) every day to and from school.

School children line up for class at Chinle Elementary School.

Love of learning, joy of life and playfulness are reflected in the faces of these Navajo pupils.

Navajo children are good learners and serious about their school work. On the other hand, the dropout rate among high school and college students is high. Contributing factors are the realization that the job market for them is very limited, and the fact that they must help with traditional chores such as sheepherding and farm work.

This third grader is hard at work, mastering his writing and reading skills.

Navajos love sports. Besides traditional games, such as shinny ball (a form of hockey) and horse racing, boys and girls enjoy all kinds of athletics. Track and field events, baseball, basketball and football are very popular. Here the Fort Defiance High School football team takes on their rivals from Tuba City.

The ultra-modern Navajo Community College is built in the shape of a six-sided hogan. The dormitories, too, are hogan-shaped. The buildings are arranged according to old-fashioned Navajo custom. Just as a medicine man occupies the place of honor when transmitting the old tribal lore inside the hogan, so the center of learning occupies the place of honor within the circle of college buildings. As the women's quarters and the cooking hearth occupy a certain spot within the hogan, so the girls' dorms and cafeteria are situated in a corresponding place within the college circle. An old-style hogan, still used for ceremonies, can be seen, dwarfed by the huge main building. Thus the Community College embodies in perfect harmony the old and the new.

Mr. Mike Mitchell, teacher and medicine man, recites to his students the age-old creation myths of the Dinneh.

Navajo teachers often use illustrations created by students to make more vivid the story of the Holy People — of Changing Woman, Spider Woman and the Hero Twins.

At the big annual tribal fair which lasts for four days children like the breathtaking rides, screaming with joy, excitement and, perhaps, also a little fear as they are whirled around.

At many Indian pow-wows the Navajos dress up as Comanches or Sioux, putting on war bonnets while performing the dances of various Plains tribes. In this way, they feel they are contributing to a brotherly feeling which embraces many tribes.

Navajo girls compete in the Miss Indian Beauty Contest—not without success.

All through the year Navajos compete in tribal rodeos. This is an exciting, but also a very dangerous sport where a young man can easily get hurt. Some of the best rodeo riders throughout the country are Indians.

Epilogue

One of the greatest of Indian problems is how to live and work in modern America and still remain a traditional Navajo. Living a dual lifestyle, half-Indian and half-white, as many of these people must, is never easy. This drawing represents the inner conflict facing these native Americans.

The Navajos are living symbols of human endurance and the will to survive. At the dawn of history they managed to survive and to adapt themselves to the harsh conditions of the Arctic wastelands. They survived the burning deserts, the muskets of the Spaniards and Kit Carson's cannon. They survived "The Long Walk" and years of captivity at Bosque Redondo—their supreme trial has been likened to the holocaust suffered by the Jewish people. They have survived the dark days of livestock reduction, the killing of their sheep on Government orders, because they had run out of grazing land. They have not only survived the onrush of white civilization, technology, and tourists, but have turned these things to their advantage while surviving as Navajos. They are still fighting for their water and their land. "As long as we hold on to that," they say, "we will endure as the Dinneh—the people."

The Navajos survived "The Long Walk" to Fort Sumner in 1866. One sign of their survival, not only of the body but also of the spirit, can be seen in the bright, shining faces of Navajo children. They represent the future of the nation. It can be seen in the smoke of juniper fires at a squaw dance. It can be seen in the fact that over a thousand medicine men and women still perpetuate the ancient beliefs of the people. "We will still be here," said a young Navajo, "long after the power plants and strip mines are gone. We will still be singing our old, sacred songs, we will still walk in beauty."

These children are having a good time going to a picnic in the family pickup truck. The majority of vehicles are pickups, which are well-suited to the Indians' lifestyle. Most pickups are painted turquoise blue, the people's sacred and favorite color. This red and white one is an exception.

Navajos say: "Our greatest treasures are not coal, or oil, or uranium, but our children." In Monument Valley this beautiful little girl sells necklaces made of seeds.

It is fun to be a Navajo child, in spite of hardships. Navajos are gentle parents who never beat, and only rarely scold, their children. This warm, loving relationship is reflected in the children's smiles.

Walking in beauty in a beautiful land—that is the Navajo way.

"In beauty I walk.
With the pollen of dawn upon my path
I wander.
With beauty before me, I walk.
With beauty behind me, I walk.
On the trail of morning, I walk."

About the Author

Originally Viennese, Richard Erdoes studied art at the Academy of Vienna, Berlin and the Académie de la Grande-Chaumiere in Paris. Driven out of Europe by the Nazis, Erdoes came to New York in 1940. For the next 30 years he worked in that city as a free-lance artist and illustrator. His work appeared in *Life, Time, Fortune, The Saturday Evening Post, American Heritage, The New York Times* and many other major publications. Erdoes wrote and illustrated a dozen children's books for MacMillan, McGraw-Hill, Random House and Dodd, Mead & Co. He also painted murals and produced educational films. Under the influence of some of the great *Life* photographers he also took up photography as a second profession. Erdoes' work has been exhibited and reviewed both in the United States and in Europe. At Time, Inc., he met his wife Jean, a Pennsylvania-born artist and art director. They have two boys and one girl.

Painting assignments for various magazines led to trips to Indian reservations. These resulted in close friendships with a number of Native American families. For almost twenty years the Erdoes family has spent weeks and months with their Indian friends, both at the Erdoes home in New York and on the reservations. During the Sixties and Seventies Richard and Jean became deeply involved in the Indian civil rights struggle. Out of this experience came a number of books, among them: "Lame Deer, Seeker of Visions" (Simon & Schuster), "The Sun Dance People," "The Rain Dance People," and "The Sound of Flutes" (all Alfred A. Knopf). Richard Erdoes also had his first novel "A Woman Who Dared" published by Fawcett. Richard and Jean Erdoes now make their home in Santa Fe, New Mexico, surrounded by Indian pueblos and the majesty of Navajo land.

INDEX